RAW EGG NATIONALISM In Theory and Practice

Cook Good with the Raw Egg Nationalist

This is not a book of philosophy or an exhortation. It is just a collection of the thoughts and opinions of someone who has been practising raw egg nationalism for some time now. I'm not trying to convert you. The choice is yours.

If you do decide to try the raw egg lifestyle, your brand will not look entirely like mine – and that's a good thing. From the start, this has been an esoteric movement of likeminded individuals, as well as a crossover with other worthy politico-ethical causes like raw milk nationalism, raw meat nationalism, café racer nationalism, handsome Thursday, fonky monky Friday, and open borders for hotties. Our diversity is, and always will be, our strength. There is no single way.

The book begins with an introduction to raw egg nationalism and is then followed by a series of recipes, including the OG or 'Original Gironda' raw egg shake, other raw and cooked egg recipes and various steak-related recipes. The book ends with some treats and cocktails. All of the recipes, except the steak sauces, have some egg component to them.

One last thing. Make sure to follow: Ben Braddock (@autistlvsmatter), Chris Hardman (@chhardman), Scaevola (@Scaevolacordus), PWAM Spartan (@SolaryanSpartan), Classic Age Vitalist (@CVitalist), Jawbrah (@ZyzzRespecter), Landshark (@LandsharkRides), Lord Bull Carson, esq. (@BillCarsonII), Chris Benoit III (@Benoitreturn)…

…Too many names to name. In time, you will come to know them all, and like me you will benefit from the kindness of these wise and generous souls.

The Virgin Meal Prepper

Chicken or beef + sweet potato ad nauseam

8.30 alarm, go get coffee
8.50 cardio
10 meal prep
10.30 eat meal 1, shower prep for work
13.00 eat meal 2
14.00 gym and cardio
17.00 eat meal 3
18.00 work
19.00 eat meal at work fast
21.30 eat meal 5
22.30 finish accounts and go home
23.30 eat meal
00.30 sleep and repeat

Cooks his food in a non-stick frying pan

Posts photos of his scuffed tupperware on Instagram

Wears a weight belt and straps for every exercise

Claims to weigh 80kg

5'5"

Scoffs his tepid unseasoned bacteria-ridden food in between waves of customers at the Indian restaurant where he works

Believes eggs are bad for you because muh cholesterol

The Chad Egg Slonker

Pays no heed to the time of day

Adds raw eggs to raw milk, heavy cream and maple syrup

His dairy-rich diet is perfectly suited to his ancestral genetics, which found their first expression on the Pontic steppe 4,000 years ago

crack *crack* *crack* *crack* *crack* *crack* *SLURRRPPPPPP*

OUCH!

Never gets tired of drinking what is essentially a gourmet milkshake

Slonks his egg tonic from a stylish glass milk bottle

Laughs off questions from greasy manosphere grifters about the greater bioavailability of cooked egg protein by pointing to the incredible androgenic effects of massive consumption of cholesterol, which is denatured by heat

Get yolk if you want to be yoked

Gains fifty pounds in under a year

Leads a revolution in animal welfare by insisting on only the highest quality eggs sourced locally from free-range pasture-raised chickens

A WORD OR TWO ABOUT RAW EGG NATIONALISM

A Word or Two about Raw Egg Nationalism

Raw egg nationalism. It's in the name. Raw eggs + nationalism = raw egg nationalism. A physical and political ethic built upon the massive consumption of raw eggs.

Huh?

My friend Ben Braddock (formerly @benbraddock67, and @autistlvsmatter, now @graduatedben) wrote very eloquently about raw egg nationalism recently in an article.

> *The premise is simple really, we are nationalists of a variety that emphasize the health and vitality of the nation-state and all who live in it. The corrupted toxic food supply is an outgrowth of the large-scale low-quality mindset of globalism that has no concern other than the bottom line. No loyalty to the health and vitality of the country or anyone in it.*[1]

There we have explained, succinctly, the relationship between nationalism and physical health, as it stands today. The nationalists, us, and our enemy – the forces of globalism and the planetary race to the bottom they are pursuing. In the name

---

[1] https://countere.com/home/raw-egg-nationalism

of unimaginable wealth for themselves, just a tiny minority of the world population, the globalists immiserate and enfeeble everybody else; a process that will lead, if unchecked, to a world of cities that resemble the worst of present-day India – shining citadels of the rich surrounded by vast teeming slums of filth – and the replacement of the natural world in its infinite variety and beauty by Frankenstein monoculture and monstrous factory warehouses where animals are housed and processed without a thought for their dignity as sentient creatures, a landscape marred and poisoned by genetically modified crops, pesticides, insecticides and enormous pools of festering animal waste. Nationalism is the only effective way to resist this; anything else seems, ultimately, to be surrender. By strengthening the nation state, we make possible the strengthening of the individual, and indeed nature herself, in a way that is at the very least inimical to, if not impossible under, the rule of globalism.

This attitude is only natural. Numerous studies have been written about the effects of physical fitness on political outlook. But did we need sociologists to tell us that an activity – the physical cult, in all its forms – that emphasises self-reliance,

11

self-overcoming, discipline, dedication and pain as the true path to beauty and understanding would almost exclusively be the province of men (and women) of the right? Anything with even the slightest whiff of independence, of the impudent suggestion of hierarchy, is toxic to the left (the useful idiots of globalism), who want you weak, dependent upon all sorts of products of perverted science, submerged into a formless mass of mere flesh, just like in that horrible '80s video nasty, *Society*. The rare attempt of the left to recognise that it might at least be of practical value to have some men of action among its ranks, as in the recent 'swole left' meme, is destined to end in pathetic failure. Once you shake off the physical chains of the modern world and the modern left – as you become fit and beautiful – so you must necessarily shake off their mental chains too. And so, of course, they don't want you to be fit, or beautiful.

Okay. But what do raw eggs have to do with it?

Eggs are important to raw egg nationalists both as a symbol and as a food of immense nutritional value. The symbolic, indeed esoteric, aspect I won't go into much here, suffice to say that since time immemorial the egg has represented, variously, the created world; the cycle of birth, death and rebirth; the sun; the sexual act; and much more besides.[2] The dichotomy raw-cooked is also of important symbolic meaning too, capturing the eternal interface between nature and culture, between the powers beyond us and the powers within us as humans, between the mute world in-itself and the concepts we create to understand it – the world as will and the world as representation.[3] A symbol of the generative power of nature, the raw egg, when consumed, symbolically returns us to a nature from which the modern world alienates us. But perhaps I have already said too much, for these are secrets that are revealed to the initiate only with time...

So let me speak about the nutritional value of eggs and why they are so important to us, the raw egg nationalists. You may already suspect that the vast majority of what passes for 'nutritional advice' today is nonsense; you wouldn't be here otherwise, would you? The so-called food pyramid: eat grains, legumes and vegetables, and avoid red meat, dairy and saturated fats. The recommended daily calorie intake: just look

---

[2] I suggest you read George Bataille's *Story of the Eye* to see this symbolism explored.

[3] See Claude Lévi-Strauss, *The Raw and the Cooked* (New York, 1969).

after the numbers and the rest will look after itself; 2000 calories is 2000 calories, regardless of where you get them from. No single food, perhaps apart from butter, has been subject to greater calumnies in our time than the egg. Even bodybuilders, engaged in the most anabolic activity known to man, have swallowed the anti-egg propaganda hook, line and sinker: the beastliest gymbro will turn into a quivering girly-man at the thought of consuming more than a single egg yolk a day. But why? The answer lies in a single word: cholesterol. The average egg contains nearly 200mg of cholesterol, most of it in the yolk, and the recommended daily allowance is just 300mg. Too much cholesterol in the diet leads to too much cholesterol in the blood, which inevitably leads, or so we are told, to a heart attack and death. And as for *raw* eggs, well, you don't want a side of salmonella to go with your heart attack, do you?

Poppycock.

Balderdash.

Drivel.

14

Shite.

Utter shite, in fact. 'You have been lied to your entire life', Braddock says – and he is totally right. In truth, cholesterol is an essential component of the diet; where cholesterol goes wrong is when you consume large amounts of polyunsaturated fatty acids (often referred to as PUFAs) in your diet, which oxidise easily and cause all sorts of nasty cell damage and even cancer.[4] Most importantly of all for us raw egg nationalists, cholesterol is one of the building blocks of anabolic hormones, and that includes the all-important testosterone. The conversion rate of dietary cholesterol to testosterone stands at as much as 10%. Indeed, cholesterol consumption shows a stronger correlation with lean muscle mass increase than protein intake.[5] The eggs must be raw, because heating damages the cholesterol, making it less readily usable in the body; as long as the eggs are good quality – a point I'll return to – the risk of salmonella is close to zero. This

---

[4] The nutritionist Ray Peat has written extensively about the negative health effects of PUFAs.

[5] See, for instance, Riechman et al., 'Statins and dietary and serum cholesterol are associated with increased lean mass following resistance training', *The Journals of Gerontology. Series A, Biological and Medical Sciences*, 62:10 (200), 1164-71.

is where the incomprehension of poolboy manosphere grifters is at its most acutely revealing. 'But, bro, the protein in eggs has a greater bioavailability when they're cooked. LOL dumbass. (Buy my Achilles Program.)' It's not primarily about the protein in the eggs, and it never has been.

All of this was well known to Vince Gironda, a man I have referred to elsewhere (use the Twitter search function) as the 'Nikola Tesla of bodybuilding'. Vince Gironda, the 'Iron Guru', was almost certainly the most innovative bodybuilder and physique coach of the so-called Golden Era of bodybuilding. Bodybuilders from across the world, including a young and still-green Arnold, sought him out for his trademark programmes, exercises and diets: the 10x10, 8x8, and 10, 8, 6, 15; the sissy squat, drag curl and frog crunch; the steak and eggs diet, the liver-tablet diet and the 36-raw-eggs a day, or 'hormone precursor' diet. A man of great power and will, Gironda famously dismissed Arnold as a 'fat fuck' upon his first arriving at his gym; a bit harsh, perhaps, but under Gironda's tutelage, Arnold would take his physique to the next level, paving the way for his multiple Mr Olympia wins. In his own time as a bodybuilder during the 1950s and '60s,

Gironda's magnificently shredded and classically proportioned physique stood out a country mile from his peers; although he was actually penalised and lost out on titles for being *too ripped and defined,* at a time when a softer, rounder musculature was favoured. Sadly, for some reason, Gironda fell out of favour and has never really received the recognition he deserved for his pathbreaking approaches – hence the Tesla moniker. Perhaps he was just too far ahead of the curve, too brilliant; his uncompromising character, and willingness to say things others didn't want to hear, can hardly have helped either.

Of all Gironda's innovations in the world of fitness, it is the 36-raw-eggs-a-day diet, and the rationale behind it, that most interests us as raw egg nationalists.[6] Again, the key is in the name: the diet involves, quite simply, eating 36 raw eggs a day. Just that number of eggs alone, assuming they are medium eggs, has a volume of 1.5 litres. To make them more palatable and easier to consume, Gironda advocated taking them in three doses of what is essentially a gourmet milkshake, as I like to

---

[6] Here I draw on the fantastic series of videos on Gironda and his diets by Youtuber Golden Era Bookworm. His channel contains a wealth of info. (https://www.youtube.com/channel/UCP37ob25oGKxrKEQFiZGArA).

call it, a kind of anabolic custard: 12 eggs mixed with milk and heavy cream in a 1:1 ratio (referred to as 'half and half'), perhaps with honey or maple syrup as flavouring. That's a whopping 7.2g of cholesterol from just the eggs, enough to give the average know-nothing general practitioner a heart attack just from hearing about it. Gironda's claim was that a cycle of these milkshakes – for 36 eggs a day was not to be a constant intake – is a close as the natural lifter can get to a cycle of steroids without taking steroids; off the cycle, the lifter might consume a more reasonable number of raw eggs a day, such as 12 or 18. Here, as elsewhere, Gironda's claims were not merely anecdotal but backed up by readings from a wide variety of literature, including scientific papers of the time and also accounts of explorers like Vilhjalmur Stefansson who had spent time in the Arctic Circle with the Inuit, observing and following their high fat and protein diet. Gironda knew that at the beginning of the 20th century, it had been common practice to give burns victims a diet of 36 eggs a day, in various forms, not only raw (in shakes or ice cream) but also cooked, to counter the terrible muscle wastage that results from burn damage to soft tissue. Two studies from the mid-1960s, with which he may have been familiar, suggested that the massive

18

egg consumption had been mimicking the effects of newly available steroids like dianabol, which by that time had replaced the egg diet for burns victims in hospital. In addition to the hormonal effects, about which Gironda was well aware, the studies claimed that massive egg consumption, like the use of dianabol, also helped to maintain a positive nitrogen balance throughout the day, which is essential for lean muscle retention and growth.

But of course, there will be doubters. The evidence for the efficacy of the diet, if by evidence you mean peer-reviewed scientific studies, is not exactly overwhelming. In the world of fitness and nutrition, though, the gold standard is often not the scientific literature, which may in fact be hopelessly confused or just downright wrong, but the tried and tested anecdotal evidence of others who have manifested the results you are seeking to achieve. Tetchy old boomer he may be, writer of appalling weightlifting-themed internet erotica, but like your uncle Mark Rippetoe also knows a thing or two about what is and isn't bullshit.

A Word or Two about Raw Egg Nationalism

We all know that 40 milligrams of Dianabol a day is a pretty effective dose for a weightlifter. How many peer-reviewed studies support this? Zero. How many anecdotal reports? About a hundred thousand. You're an idiot if you avoid anecdotal data, pure and simple.[7]

Look at Vince Gironda himself. Look at his tremendous physique. Then look at the tremendous physiques of the men he trained. Arnold Schwarzenegger. Larry Scott. Lou Ferrigno. Frank Zane. Vinnie must have been on to something (or *on something*, I hear you quip. YES: RAW EGGS). There are the testimonies of raw-egg Twitter too, including myself and the many people I follow and who follow me. And unlike many named and anonymous accounts, we aren't trying to sell you anything. The fitness plans and the diets we follow (like those of the masculinity-conference grifters) are freely available online; the difference between us and them is that we aren't cynically repackaging any of it – altering set numbers or exercises orders slightly from a plan we found on /fit/, adding in one or two extra exercises – and asking money for our minimal effort. It makes no difference to us, at least not

---

[7] https://www.t-nation.com/training/most-lifters-are-still-beginners

materially, whichever way you choose. That being said, I'd like to issue a little challenge to all the naysayers, the people who think this is all 'just a meme': if you consider yourself a devotee of the path of sun and steel but you aren't prepared to try even a single cycle of raw egg nationalism, why are you even here? If anything embodies the Faustian spirit of being at once the experimenter and the matter experimented upon, it is bodybuilding. Chet Yorton insisting on doing three sets of 22 reps for every exercise. Vince Gironda eating 150 liver tablets a day for two weeks. A young Arnold squatting late into the night in the Austrian forest with his friends, waking up the next day and finding himself unable to stand. Mike Mentzer's diet of amphetamines and ice cream. The list of oddballs is as long as the list of the greatest and best, because the greatest and best are and always have been prepared to experiment on themselves. They put it all on the line, knowing there was no single way; the truth was theirs to find. The first time I heard about the diet, I thought 'crazy. I've got to try it.' So try it. At worst, you'll end up spending less than you were spending on inferior quality protein powder; and unlike with that whey protein isolate, you *won't* get awful wind. At best, you might start making serious gains and you might learn something about yourself.

And you can do your part for the benefit of animal welfare at the same time. How? By insisting on only the best quality eggs, from happy, well-treated animals. It's a truism that you are what you eat; and that extends to how what you eat, eats and lives too. On nutritional, as well as ethical grounds, the raw egg nationalist insists on eggs that come from hens that spend their time outdoors, clucking and pecking and foraging in the dirt and grass; not animals confined by the tens of thousand to striplit barns, destined to live their short painful lives covered in their own filth, fed and watered by machines, starved of sunlight and stimulation. If the bugman wishes to live that way, crammed in his pod – let him; but no hen would choose a life of confinement like that. One day, the great evils of factory farming will be avenged, and the blood of the mass-murder profiteers will run through the streets... I digress. Optimally, unless you have your own pampered hens, you'll go to a farm that sells its own eggs and as you cross the yard you'll see the hens being birbs, just as they should be. If not, insist on free-range, organic, pasture-raised eggs and be prepared too, to look into what those terms actually mean; often, it is not what you think it is.

Well, that's it for this introduction. I don't want to say too much and be too prescriptive. As I said elsewhere, raw egg nationalism is a practice of esoteric self-realisation; ultimately, it is a path of self-discovery you must walk yourself. I am not a guide, merely a fellow traveller.

SHAKES

THE "OG": ORIGINAL GIRONDA EGG SHAKE[8]

This is where it all begins: the Gironda shake.

The OG.

Simple.

Delicious.

Anabolic.

Gironda's original programme, the 'hormone precursor diet', involved cycling up to three shakes of 12 eggs a day for a month, over a six-to-eight-week period. In addition, he advocated a pill regimen to accompany the shakes that would make even an AIDS sufferer balk; I won't go into much detail about the supplements here.[9]

---

[8] The information here comes, again, from various excellent videos by Golden Era Bookworm.

[9] The regimen consisted of: one multivitamin, one zinc tablet, five alfalfa tablets, ten kelp tablets, three wheatgerm tablets, one RNA-DNA tablet, one HCL tablet, three digestive tablets, three lysine tablets and three multi-glandular tablets. Gironda also suggested taking ten liver tablets every three

The recipe for Gironda's original shake is as follows:

- 12 whole eggs
- 350ml half and half (milk and heavy cream in equal quantities)
- 1/3 cup of milk and egg protein powder
- A banana (to taste).

Vince advocated 'fertilised' eggs, which basically meant free-range, not battery, eggs. Of course, as you'd expect, he was aware that the nutritional quality of eggs depends on the quality of the animals that lay them.

The full eight-week cycle would look like this:

Week one: shake for breakfast; 1lb meat and salad for lunch; 1lb meat and salad for dinner.

Week two: shake for breakfast; 1lb meat and salad for lunch; another shake as a snack; 1lb meat and salad for dinner.

---

hours, five yeast tablets with each protein drink, four orchic tissue (i.e. bull's testicle) tablets before and after each workout, and six tryptophan and calcium tablets before bed.

Weeks three to six: shake for breakfast; 1lb meat and salad for lunch; another shake as a snack; 1lb meat and salad for dinner; a third shake.

Week seven: same as week two.

Week eight: same as week one.

You'll recognise this as a high-protein-and-fat, low-carb diet. Gironda advocated having carbs twice a week, on a Wednesday and a Saturday, with one of the meals. He recommended whole grain carbs such as oats, rice, pasta and potatoes.

Each shake works out at roughly 1800 calories, so in weeks three to six you'll be taking in 5400 calories from the shakes alone; with the meat meals included, you're looking at close to 7000 calories a day. The ease with which you can consume so many calories on the hormone precursor diet is of course one of its greatest recommendations. You only need to watch one or two 'full day's eating' videos by the likes of Brian Shaw or

Eddie Hall to see how miserable the alternative is. Pity the Virgin Meal Prepper – even if he is the world's strongest man.

SOME VARIATIONS ON THE GIRONDA SHAKE

RAW EGG NATIONALIST'S PRE- AND POST-WORKOUT SHAKES

These are the shakes I have been taking regularly for the past year or so. When the Cringe Aids pandemic began, I had to reduce my egg consumption after the local farmshop got raided and the farmer decided to limit each customer to no more than a dozen eggs at a time. At one point I was consuming as few as a nine raw eggs a day; but thankfully now I've returned to a more acceptable number, usually between 12 and 18 a day, although sometimes more. My shakes differ from Gironda's in not having the protein powder in them; only my post-workout shake has a banana (or two) in it.

- 6-12 eggs
- 350ml half and half
- maple syrup to taste

■   1-2 bananas (post-workout only)

BEN BRADDOCK'S VANILLA DELIGHT AND OJ SHAKE

Ben Braddock, a very important member of the movement, is also a fan of maple syrup in his egg shake, as well as a little splash of vanilla extract. Ben also suggests adding OJ to the shake; purist that he is, he insists on buying oranges from the store and juicing them himself. Ray Peat is a big fan of orange juice and milk together. He says

> *A daily diet that includes milk and orange juice provides fructose and other sugars for general resistance to stress, but larger amounts of fruit juice, honey and other (appropriate) sugars can protect against increased stress and can reverse some of the established degenerative conditions.*

BORIS FROM PRAGUE'S BIG DICK TONIC

My friend Boris from Prague (@BorisVonPrag) has a variation involving more fruit, usually berries in addition to bananas, and sometimes nut butter and whey protein powder. The origin of the shake's name, and any evidence that it lives up to it, is not forthcoming. Try it and see.

OTHER GOLDEN ERA SHAKES[10]

Vince Gironda wasn't the only Golden Era bodybuilder to have his own signature shake. In an era when commercially made protein powders were just beginning to hit the market, almost every bodybuilder had their own preferred recipe or recipes. Rheo Blair, a celebrity nutritionist of the time, was one of the first to market protein powder, beginning in 1951. His most famous product was Blair Protein, a mix of casein and whey protein, dried milk powder, dried whole eggs and flavouring.

---

[10] The information here is largely taken from plagueofstrength.com's article on bulking shakes from the Golden Era. Caveat lector: the website is very NSFW. The information on John McCallum is from https://www.t-nation.com/training/mccallum-s-high-protein-high-set-program .

Arnold, Franco Columbo, Ken Waller and Ric Drasin were all champions of Blair's products at one time or another. Blair had a selection of shake recipes of his own, two of which are reproduced below.

As with Gironda's shake, the focus of these Golden Era shakes was on a proper balance between protein and fat. Many of the shakes were more like puddings, with ice cubes added to thicken the mixture of powder (usually Blair's Protein), cream and other ingredients. The pudding would be eaten with a spoon throughout the day, perhaps in four or five servings; while training for his 1966 Mr Olympia title, Larry Scott ate four pounds of protein pudding a day. Blair insisted that, instead of being chugged, his protein shakes should be sipped or eaten slowly, to aid digestion.

John McCallum, the originator of the third recipe, was a well-known and respected bodybuilding writer in the 1960s and '70s, with a monthly column in *Strength and Health* magazine. He placed a particular emphasis on strength as a route to the 'power look', noting that the best developed bodybuilders of the day like John Grimek and Reg Park were also generally among the strongest. To do this he advocated heavy sets of power cleans, followed immediately by high pulls and deadlifts, with sets in the one-to-three rep range. It also meant putting on a certain amount of fat in order to maximise size and strength gains, and his 'get big' drink would provide the necessary calories, in fact an absurd amount. Note that it was intended to be taken only when the lifter was working at his hardest, and not as an everyday supplement.

BLAIR'S CREAMY DELICIOUS

- 250ml light cream
- 250ml skimmed milk
- 3 scoops of protein powder
- 1tbsp vanilla extract
- 2 eggs boiled for 30 seconds

Expect to consume about 1000 calories with this shake.

BLAIR'S CALIFORNIA COCONUT DELIGHT

- 150ml light cream

- 500ml skimmed milk

- 3 scoops of protein powder

- 2tbsp coconut extract

- 1 egg boiled for 30 seconds

This shake has a more modest 520 calories.

JOHN MCCALLUM'S 'GET BIG DRINK'

- 2ltr whole milk

- 500ml dried skimmed milk

- 6-8 scoops of protein powder

- 2 eggs

- 4tbsp peanut butter

- 500g chocolate ice cream

- 1 small banana

- 4tbsp malted milk powder

- 6tbsp corn syrup

With eight scoops of protein, this makes an insane 5300 calories. Most of us would, quite rightly, sooner drink glyphosate than corn syrup – which, incidentally, is banned in the UK. Try maple syrup or honey instead.

Also try using your own home-made ice cream from one of the two recipes in the 'Treats' section.

COOKED EGGS

SCRAMBLED EGGS (AND HOW NOT TO FUCK THEM UP)

One unfortunate habit of the inexperienced cook is to move whatever is cooking (eggs, steak…) around and around the pan as it's cooking, in a manner not unlike a cat attempting to coax life back into a dead mouse. In both cases, it doesn't work. So why do it? On the cook's part, I'm sure it stems from a lack of confidence, especially if nothing *seems* to be happening in the pan; a lack of patience too, I suspect. Then there's the question of heat in the pan, something a great many people misunderstand. They turn the heat up far too high, see that the food they're cooking is being incinerated, and think that by moving it constantly around they'll be able to prevent it from being ruined.

So, when cooking scrambled eggs:

Don't have the heat up too high. Use a low-to-medium heat. When you add the butter to the pan it should melt and then begin to froth, but not darken. If your pan is too hot, the butter will quickly boil and then burn, leaving horrible black particles in the pan. The eggs, once in the pan, should sizzle and then bubble, but not boil.

Don't move the eggs around too much. The method I advocate basically involves treating the eggs in the pan like an omelette. Once you've poured them in, don't do anything with them until they've formed the beginning of an omelette – i.e. a solid layer – on the bottom of the pan, with liquid eggs on top. Then begin to draw the eggs into the centre of the pan, forming thick, creamy folds. Then wait for a solid layer to form again and repeat. Instead of a grainy texture, you'll end up with big folds of cooked egg, especially if you add a little milk or cream to the recipe, as I suggest. A very useful piece of kit for this method is a rubber or silicon spatula.

Don't season the scrambled eggs until you serve them. If you season the eggs while they're cooking, they'll weep, leaving you with dry eggs sat in a puddle of water.

This recipe is a good size serving for a hungry boy. A medium-sized pan is necessary. In a small pan, it will take too long to cook (because the liquid will be too deep in the pan), and in a large, it will cook too quickly (because the liquid will be too spread out).

- Four eggs
- A dash of whole milk or heavy cream
- A knob of butter
- Salt and pepper

Add the butter to a pan on a low-to-medium heat and swirl to coat the pan. Beat the eggs gently and then add the milk or cream. When the butter froths, add the eggs. The eggs should sizzle a little. Wait for a solid layer to form and then begin to draw the eggs in from the outside to the centre of the pan with a spatula to create large folds. Allow the eggs to solidify for a moment again, and then do the same again with the spatula. Keep doing this – waiting for a solid layer and then drawing it in – until the eggs are done: the folds should still be creamy when you serve the eggs. Season with salt and pepper once the egg is on the plate.

Try adding a few splashes of Tabasco as the eggs are cooking.

Scrambled eggs and smoked salmon is a classic combination. I'd suggest adding some black pudding or other blood sausage (e.g. boudin noir) too. Layer smoked salmon on a fried slice of the pudding or sausage and then pour the cooked eggs over the top. If you're feeling especially gastronomic, garnish with some freshly chopped chives.

POACHED EGGS

There's nothing complicated about poaching eggs. Just a few tips will help you.

Fresher eggs will hold a round shape better as they cook, because the white will be thicker and adhere to the yolk better. If your egg isn't fresh, crack it into a bowl and drain off the runnier part of the white. Crack the egg into a bowl or a cup. This makes it easier to get the egg into the pan. Once the water in the pan is simmering, stir it to create a whirlpool in the centre. The water should not be boiling hard: if the water is moving too vigorously, it will throw the egg around and you'll end up with a stringy poached egg instead of a perfectly round one. Pour the egg into the whirlpool and let it cook for 3-4 minutes. Lift out with a slotted spoon. If there are any stringy bits, they can be removed with scissors or a knife.

OMELETTES

Here's a simple omelette recipe. The most common difficulties experienced when making an omelette involve folding it and getting it out of the pan in one piece. I wouldn't recommend using a non-stick pan, because of all the gay chemicals in the coating, which of course end up in your food; a number of studies suggest that perfluorinated compounds found in water-resistant clothing and non-stick pans can affect the body's steroid hormones, and can act like estrogen in the body, as well as probably being carcinogenic. (I'd strongly suggest investing in some decent cookware: Ebay and Etsy have vintage copper cookware at decent prices.) So long as you use a generous knob of butter, the omelette shouldn't stick. I discuss various fillings underneath the main recipe.

- 3 eggs
- Knob of butter (about a tablespoon)
- Salt and pepper

Whisk together the eggs gently until just mixed, then season. Heat the pan on a medium flame and add the butter, swirling it to coat the pan. When the butter has begun to foam, pour in the eggs, which should sizzle. Let the eggs cook for 30 seconds, then add the filling (if any). Shake the pan to distribute the eggs and filling, and tilt so that the liquid runs to the edges. The omelette should still be a little runny when you take it off the heat. Fold one side into the middle, then the other, and turn the omelette onto a warm plate.

Various kinds of cheese work well as fillings, especially cheddar or gruyere. Be careful if you use blue cheese not to use too much; as I say in my no-churn ice cream recipe below, a little funk goes a long way. Blue cheese goes well with cubed pear in an omelette. Make sure to grate or crumble the cheese before adding it. 50-75g of cheese will be enough.

If you want to add bacon or pancetta to your omelette (cheese and bacon is great), make sure to dice the bacon first and fry it until crisp.

Likewise, if you want to add onions, make sure you soften them in butter, on a low heat, first. Rather than slicing them finely, I'd suggest slicing the onion in half and then into long strands. Cheese, bacon and onion all go nicely together. If you fancy a little spice, add some jalapenos too, or, alternatively, add some Tabasco to the eggs themselves.

Spinach also makes a great addition to an omelette. The spinach won't need to be wilted beforehand: the steam from the cooking omelette will be sufficient. The same is true for other salad leaves like rocket. Ask Spinach Brah (@BasedSpinach) if you want to know the benefits of eating spinach, which are many.

You can overload your omelette as much as you want, but the more overloaded it becomes, the more difficult it will be to fold it and get it out of the pan in one piece.

FISHERMAN'S EGGS

One of the principal ingredients of fisherman's eggs, besides the eggs, is sardines, aka 'deenz'. As well as being convenient to store, cheap and tasty, deenz are high in protein, omega-3 fatty acids and essential vitamins and minerals; because the deen is a small fish, lower down the food chain, it is also less susceptible to contaminants, including mercury, than other larger fish, such as tuna.

In this recipe, eggs are baked on top of a mix of sardines, onion, tomatoes, olives and garlic.

- Tin of sardines, in tomato sauce or olive oil
- 2 whole eggs
- 1/2 red onion, diced
- 1 large tomato, seeded and diced
- 2 cloves of garlic, minced
- 1/2tbsp Kalamata olives, finely chopped
- Handful of fresh parsley, chopped
- Salt and pepper

Preheat oven to 350F. Heat olive oil in an ovenproof pan on a medium heat. Add the onions and soften them for a few minutes, keeping them moving with a spoon or spatula to prevent them from browning. Add the tomatoes, garlic and olives and cook for a further 3 or 4 minutes. Add the sardines and break them up with a fork. Mix the contents of the pan together well and season. Continue to cook for five minutes. Crack the eggs on top of the mixture and bake in the oven for 8-10 minutes, until the egg whites have set. Garnish with the parsley.

A glug of hot sauce wouldn't go amiss here.

SHAKSHOUKA

This Mediterranean dish isn't too dissimilar from fisherman's eggs: baked eggs on a vegetable base. Shakshouka is spicier than fisherman's eggs – unless you go crazy with the hot sauce – and doesn't contain any fish or meat. Shakshouka can be eaten any time of the day (how brunch!).

Be careful not to use a cast-iron pan, unless it's very well-seasoned: the tomatoes will eat away at the seasoning. You'll need an ovenproof pan.

To peel fresh tomatoes easily, put them in a jug, pour boiling water over them, leave them for a minute, then pour off the boiling water. The skin will slide off easily.

This will make enough for two, or for one hungry raw egg nationalist.

- 1/2 white onion, diced
- 1/2 red bell pepper, seeded and diced
- 2 cloves of garlic, minced
- 2tsp paprika
- 1tsp cumin
- 1/2 tin of tomatoes, or three large fresh tomatoes, peeled and finely chopped
- Salt and pepper
- 3 whole eggs
- Handful of fresh coriander, chopped
- Handful of fresh parsley, chopped

Preheat oven to 350F. Heat olive oil in a pan on medium heat. Add pepper and onion and cook for 5 minutes, stirring to prevent from browning. Add garlic and spices and cook for a further minute or two. Add the tinned or fresh tomatoes and break them up using a wooden spoon. Season with salt and pepper and then bring the sauce to a simmer and cook for 5 minutes. Make three wells for the eggs in the sauce and crack the eggs into them. Put the pan in the oven for 8-10 minutes, until the egg whites are set. Garnish with the coriander and parsley and serve from the pan.

You can also crumble cheese into shakshouka. For authenticity, I'd recommend a goat's cheese like feta, but cheddar or a similar cheese is just fine. Blue cheese is a no-no. Add the cheese when you add the eggs

STEAK

Steak

Good quality red meat and organ meat are, of course, essential parts of raw egg nationalism. It should go without saying that high-quality animal protein is essential for anybody looking to make gains. Gironda advocated two meals of a pound of red meat a day as part of his hormone precursor diet, as well as copious amounts of liver tablets. Generally, I have cold meat and cheese for lunch, and then a large piece of steak for dinner every night, with a slice or two of liver and also some blood ('black') pudding. Despite the incredulity of the women in my life, I never get bored of eating the same, simple food every day. Tacitus could have been describing me when he wrote that the ancient Germans, unlike the Romans, were satisfied with simple foods – 'rustic fruits, fresh meat and congealed milk. They banish hunger without preparation or blandishments'. 'My ancestor!'

Again, the emphasis with your red meat, as with your eggs, should be on quality. Aim for grass-fed meat, ideally from a local butcher. Grass-fed as opposed to grain-fed beef has a better ratio of Omega-3 to Omega-6 and is richer in various vitamins and minerals, including vitamin E. Remember too that, if for whatever reason you can only get bad-quality beef, lamb is always grass-fed; occasionally, though, lamb, especially American lamb, may be finished with grain feed in a feedlot.

In this section I'll discuss another of Gironda's diets, the steak-and-eggs diet, which he also called the 'maximum definition diet', I'll provide some recipes for simple accompaniments for steak, and also a recipe for steak tartare, which is traditionally served with a single raw egg yolk and may very well be your first experience of the power of raw meat nationalism. If you haven't already, look up Aajonus Vonderplanitz; Jawbrah (@ZyzzRespecter) and Landshark (@LandsharkRides) both have lots of useful information about him.

A NOTE ON GIRONDA'S STEAK-AND-EGGS DIET

Gironda called this diet the 'maximum definition diet'. Again, as with the 36-eggs-a-day diet, it's in the name: you eat a big plate of steak and eggs, twice a day – and that's it. It's basically a low-carb, ketogenic diet (well ahead of the curve once again), and Gironda himself used it to get in shape before contest –

remember, he was so shredded that he was actually penalised in competition – and he also used to advocate it for his clients looking to lose body fat and gain lean muscle. If you're looking to cut weight, try it for two or three weeks and then decide whether or not to continue it for longer.

The steak can be cooked any way you choose, and the same goes for the eggs: boiled, fried, scrambled, in an omelette, or raw. You can eat the two meals whenever you like, so this routine would fit in well with a schedule of intermittent fasting, e.g. you have your first meal at midday and then your second before 8pm, so that you're running a 16/8 split. There's no calorie counting, either: eat as much as you want, until you feel sated. On the fourth day, you should eat a carb meal to replenish your glycogen stores.

A FEW ACCOMPANIMENTS TO STEAK

There's no reason ever to get bored eating steak. Here are a couple of recipes for simple accompaniments to steak that can be made in minutes.

SIMPLE PEPPERCORN SAUCE

This is a very simple and delicious sauce for steak – a classic. It's also a good way to make liver more palatable, if you're eating it with your steak. The sauce is made in the same pan as the steak you're cooking, when you've removed the steak from the pan to let it rest for a few minutes; you will, of course, be cooking your steak with good-quality butter, on a heat that doesn't cause the butter to burn. Heat control, as I've said earlier, is crucial, and never more than when you're cooking with butter. People assume, wrongly, that in order to get a crust on a piece of steak, you have to cook it on a hellish heat, but in reality a medium heat – the butter will brown and froth but not under any circumstances be smoking – is all you need. Don't push the steak around the pan: leave it where it is until you're going to flip it.

The sauce involves a quick flambé. It's easier to do with a long match than a lighter. Don't be scared, homie.

- 1tbsp black peppercorns
- 1 glug of whisky or rum

- 150ml heavy cream
- Salt and pepper (ground)

When you flip your steak, add the peppercorns to the pan to soften. When your steak is ready, take it out of the pan and place on a hot plate to rest. Pour in the whisky or rum and light with a long match. Once the flames have disappeared, pour in the heavy cream and swirl the pan to cover it. Bring up to a boil and then turn down the heat and let the sauce simmer for 3 or 4 minutes. Season and serve.

CHEAT'S BEARNAISE

To go with your cheat curls – you are doing cheat curls, aren't you, anon? (If not, go to Lindy Fit's account (@LindyFit) to find out why you should be) – here's a very simple cheat's recipe for Bearnaise sauce. This can be cooked in the same pan as the steak; as with the peppercorn sauce, you make the Bearnaise in the butter you've cooked the steak in while the steak is resting. Good things come to those who cheat.

- 1tbsp red wine vinegar

- 2tbsp crème fraîche
- 1tbsp wholegrain mustard
- 1tbsp chopped fresh tarragon
- Salt and pepper

Take steak out of the pan and place on a hot plate. Turn down the heat to low and add the vinegar, then stir in the crème fraîche and mustard. Stir until they make a sauce. Add in the tarragon and season.

TZATZIKI

Greek cooking really doesn't get the rep it deserves. Much depends, of course, on the setting; it's never quite the same if you aren't *there*. A little Greek Taverna on the water, cooled by a gentle breeze, the salt smell of the sea in your nostrils, the taste of ouzo, a dark and mysterious woman... The next time you're thinking of cooking a joint of meat, in the oven or on the barbecue, try making lamb kleftiko, with a piece of shoulder or leg. The name derives from the venerable Greek practice of sheep-stealing: the bandits themselves were known as klephts, and would cook their ill-gotten gains in pits underground, to avoid detection. When removed, after many hours of slow cooking with vegetables and herbs, the meat would simply fall apart.

Tzatziki is a simple yoghurt-based sauce that goes well with all manner of Greek-style meat, such as lamb souvlaki (kebabs), but also with steak.

- 1/2 large cucumber, skin removed and finely chopped
- 400g full-fat Greek yoghurt or other plain full-fat yoghurt or kefir
- 2 garlic cloves, minced
- 2tbsp extra virgin olive oil
- 1tbsp lemon juice
- 1/2tsp sea salt
- 1tbsp fresh dill, finely chopped, or dried dill

Mix all the ingredients and stir well to ensure they are fully combined. Refrigerate and serve cold.

CHIMICHURRI

This was one of the first recipes I posted on Twitter. It was well received, as it should have been: chimichurri is one of the ultimate accompaniments for steak, from the land of the gaucho – Argentina. Chimichurri can be used as a marinade for meat as well as a sauce.

As with the recipe I posed on Twitter, I won't give specific quantities. Taste as you go along – a general principle you should follow. There should be more parsley than oregano and garlic combined. There should be enough olive oil that the greenery is saturated but not swimming, then enough lemon juice to cut through nicely. Add chilli flakes to suit your taste.

- Fresh parsley, chopped
- Fresh oregano, chopped
- Wild garlic or garlic cloves, minced
- Chilli flakes
- Extra virgin olive oil
- Lemon juice
- Sea salt and pepper

Add olive oil to the leaves and garlic and mix. Add lemon juice, chilli flakes and seasoning.

STEAK TARTARE: BEGINNER'S RAW MEAT NATIONALISM

I will never forget my first taste of steak tartare (so-called because the Mongols, or 'Tartars', used to ride with raw meat under their saddles, which by the end of the ride would be tenderised by the pressure and warmth, and ready to eat). It was in the Astoria Hotel, in St Petersburg; I was 17 or 18. When I think of BAP's 'I must live a certain way' meme, this is what I think of: sitting in a grand 19th century ballroom, a string quartet playing in the corner; a statuesque Brigitte Nielsen blonde approaches the table with a wooden board upon which are arrayed the various ingredients – the beef, the shallots, the gherkins, the capers; 'Are the ingredients to the gentleman's liking?'… This is just a very showy way of demonstrating that the ingredients are of the best quality and are totally fresh – which they absolutely must be. The steak can only be fillet steak, and the dish must be served cold (chill the plate too). For all its luxury though, this is very simple to make. Steak tartare is usually served with pommes frites, melba toast, fried French bread or pumpernickel bread.

- 150g beef fillet, taken straight from the fridge
- 1/2tbsp capers
- 1 small shallot, finely chopped
- 1tbsp flat-leaf parsley, chopped
- 1/2tbsp extra virgin olive oil
- 1/2 gherkin, finely chopped
- 2 dashes of Tabasco
- 1/4 tsp sea salt flakes and 10 turns of black pepper
- 1 egg yolk

Trim the meat of all fat and sinew and chop finely, either by hand or by using a food processor (use the pulse button). Put the meat in a bowl with the capers, shallots, parsley, olive oil, gherkin, Tabasco and salt and pepper. Mix lightly together with two forks, then spoon onto the centre of a chilled plate, making a neat round. Make an indentation in the top and add the egg yolk to it.

TREATS

Treats

I've called this section the 'Treats' section, containing as it does two ice-cream recipes, a bread-based recipe and a recipe for meringues; but really there's no reason why ice cream, at least, shouldn't be a regular part of your diet. Mike Mentzer, originator of the 'heavy duty' training method and owner of one of the most stacked and powerful physiques in bodybuilding history, was a champion of ice cream. Before the 1980 Mr Olympia, he was eating ice cream at least four days a week and still losing fat.

> *Every day I would wake up and see more definition and the night before I had just had an ice cream cone. I mean, it's ridiculous eating nothing but protein or tuna fish and water to get cut up. Not only is it not healthy and no fun, it's just ridiculous.*[11]

If raw egg nationalism is not about anything, it's the standard dreary tuna-chicken-rice diet of the gymbro; hell, the central food source is basically a gourmet milkshake! According to Ray Peat, ice cream is actually close to a perfect food source. It's calorically dense, containing sugar, protein, saturated fat and

---

[11] https://www.ironmanmagazine.com/heavy-duty/.

cholesterol, as well as essential calcium, which helps combat hyperthyroidism. And it's an ideal food to eat before bed, as Mentzer himself did, because the saturated fat ensures the sugar is released slowly.

Beware, though. Generally, commercially made ice creams, even expensive ones, contain a lot of crap, especially carrageenan, a thickener which is used to 'inflate' the product. Carrageenan is also used to homogenise milk. Many people, especially people of Indo-European descent, who claim to be lactose intolerant are in fact intolerant of the carrageenan that has been added to most supermarket milk; once they try raw milk, the symptoms disappear. In a lab setting, carrageenan is actually, believe it or not, used to induce inflammatory tumours (granulomas), immunodeficiency, arthritis and other inflammatory conditions in animals. And yet it continues to be used widely in the food industry... Avoid at all costs, especially since you can make delicious restaurant-quality ice cream at home, either with or without an ice cream machine. I've included two recipes here, one for a frozen custard made with an ice cream machine, and another recipe that requires no churning at all.

Treats

As far as bread goes, I feel much, much better for not eating it. As soon as I stopped about a year ago – and I hadn't been eating supermarket bread, but either homemade or bakery-bought sourdough – my general sense of wellbeing increased greatly: not only did I realise I had been experiencing bloating, albeit very mildly, but my thought processes felt clearer, my moods more stable. My carbs now derive almost entirely from milk and fruit (don't tell P.D. Mangan), especially berries and bananas. Others report similar feelings when they abandon grains. If you've read Mike Ma's *Harassment Architecture*, you'll know from the inside back cover that there is a scientific paper called 'Bread and other edible agents of mental disease', in the journal *Frontiers in Human Neuroscience*. Among the claims of the paper are the following: that gluten disregulates GABA, a neurotransmitter involved in mood regulation; that antibodies against gluten are more often found in schizophrenia and autism patients than in the general population; that the historical introduction or removal of grain products from societies has been directly linked to rising or falling rates of mental illness, respectively; that removing grains from the diets of schizophrenia patients allowed them to be moved from locked to open wards more quickly. 'An edible agent of mental disease' – that's pretty powerful stuff, no?

Sol Brah (@SolBrah), for instance, swears by sourdough bread, and others also seem not to be affected in the slightest by gluten. But even if you switch from crappy quality supermarket bread to artisan sourdough, you may still experience the same feelings of sluggishness and bloating. I think it's Ray Peat who said that, once your body has become sensitised to a compound like gluten, even if you move from a globohomo variety to something closer to what our ancestors ate (such as spelt), you're still going to experience the same symptoms. You've been guthexxed.

There's another, powerful historical, argument against the consumption of grains. Elsewhere I've mentioned James Scott's book *Against the Grain: A Deep History of the Earliest States*. Basically, his claim is that the introduction of grains as a diet staple was part and parcel of one of the greatest losses of freedom in human history. Instead of being willing participants in the formation of the first centralised grain-based agrarian societies, our ancestors resisted their incorporation into them tooth and claw; and when such early states collapsed, as they often did under political as well as environmental pressures, our ancestors were only too willing to abandon the lifestyle foisted on them by a predatory elite.

> *I wonder whether the frequent abandonment of early state centers might often have been a boon to the health and safety of their populations rather than a 'dark age' signalling the collapse of a civilization.*[12]

Under the early agrarian states, people were shorter, weaker and more prone to disease than their hunter-gatherer ancestors and other free peoples, as well as being subject to a more onerous lifestyle and the depredations of aristocracies who used their labour as a means to maintain their own customary non-settled lifestyles, rich in hunting, feasting and splendour. Indeed, this physical as well as political process has very clear and obvious parallels with the domestication of animals, and these were not lost on those who imposed it. Average Josephat of ancient Mesapotamia really was more or less cattle in the

---

[12] J.C. Scott, *Against the Grain: A Deep History of the Earliest States* (London, 2017), xiii.

eyes of the nobles who ruled over him. This attitude has echoed through the centuries. We hear it again from the Mongols, thousands of years later, in their utterly dismissive treatment of the settled agrarian populations that they conquered with such devastating speed.

> *For the Mongols, the lifestyle of the peasant seemed incomprehensible... the farmers' fields were just grasslands, as were the gardens, and the peasants were like grazing animals rather than real humans who ate meat. The Mongols referred to these grass-eating people with the same terminology that they used for cows and goats. The masses of peasants were just so many herds, and when the soldiers went out to round up their people or to drive them away, they did so with the same terminology, precision, and emotion used in rounding up yaks.*[13]

Consider not eating bread as an important part of your revolt against the domestication of the human spirit, which has been taking place since the dawn of recorded history – and still

---

[13] J. Weatherford, *Genghis Khan and the Making of the Modern World* (New York, 2004), p.92.

continues apace. Never forget that, while the Lords of Lies want you to subsist on GMO glyphosate bread, maybe with the occasional 'beyond meat' soy-slop sausage or insect burger for variety, they themselves will still be dining on the best of God's bounty – the finest Angus beef, pork from black Iberico pigs, the fowl of the air and the fish of the sea...

But these latter-day domesticators are not Mongols, fitted to rule over you by their free and noble lifestyle; and you are not cattle – at least not yet.

Embrace the eternal spirit of the Steppe!

Ahem. Still, if you fancy a bready breakfast treat, why not try my eggy-bread breakfast stack? As a treat, it certainly won't kill you or enslave you – and it does taste really good.

BEN BRADDOCK'S FROZEN PEACH CUSTARD

This is a great recipe for frozen custard, which has a slightly different, richer, taste than the ice cream most of us know. Ben is clearly a man of refined taste, because he includes a little sea salt in his recipe. Know that the route to great tasting sweetness is not necessarily through adding more sweet. This recipe requires an ice-cream machine, unless you want to undergo the laborious process of hand-churning the frozen custard; a decent machine can be purchased cheaply. Save the egg whites for meringues.

- 8 egg yolks
- 4 ripe peaches
- 500ml heavy cream
- 250ml whole milk, preferably raw
- 150ml maple syrup or honey
- Pinch of sea salt flakes

Whisk the yolks with the maple syrup and salt until the mixture begins to thicken. Heat the milk and cream in a pan until they reach boiling point and then leave to cool for at least five to ten minutes. Add the warm milk and cream into the yolk mixture, whisking constantly. Let cool and then refrigerate for two hours. Remove from the fridge and churn in ice cream machine. Chunk the peaches and add to the mixture once it has churned to a soft-serve consistency.

If you wish to try other flavours, such as vanilla or coffee, see the recipe below for my no-churn ice cream. This would almost certainly work with mascarpone too.

RAW EGG NATIONALIST'S NO-CHURN ANABOLIC ICE CREAM

If you don't have an ice cream machine, this is an extremely simple and delicious way to make ice cream. The recipe uses uncooked meringue mix to ensure the ice cream freezes evenly without the need for churning. There's no simpler way to make restaurant-quality ice cream. This should produce enough for four to six normal people, or one hungry bodybuilder on a bulking phase.

- 4 whole eggs, separated into whites and yolks
- 100g granulated sugar
- 300ml heavy cream

Whisk the egg whites in a large bowl (or use a mixer) until stiff peaks form. Whisk in the sugar gradually and continue to whisk until the whites are stiff and glossy. Whisk the cream in a separate bowl until soft peaks form. Fold together the whites, cream and yokes, as well as any flavouring (see below), until fully combined. Freeze in a plastic container for at least two hours.

For vanilla, add a teaspoon of vanilla extract.

For coffee, add a cold shot of espresso or two or three tablespoons of coffee extract or substitute, such as Camp Coffee.

For berry flavour, add 150ml of sieved berry purée.

For rum and raisin, add 100g of raisins soaked in 4tbsp rum for two hours.

If you want to make a ripple ice cream, wait at least an hour, until the ice cream has started to solidify, and then break it up, before spooning the flavouring (berries or coffee) over the ice cream and then putting it back in the freezer.

Treats

For a richer alternative, replace half of the heavy cream with mascarpone. Whip the cream as per the recipe; the mascarpone does not need to be whipped. Fold the whipped cream and mascarpone in with the other ingredients as directed. Blue cheeses also work, but be careful not to use too much. A little funk goes a long way.

As a showstopper dessert, serve mascarpone or vanilla ice cream with a hot salted caramel sauce. For extra theatre – I've done this to great effect – for your dinner guest or guests, prepare the sauce in front of them, and pour it straight over their ice cream from the pan; obviously this is easier if you are eating in or near the kitchen. I recommend practising the sauce beforehand, because once caramel is ruined, it's ruined – and you don't want to embarrass yourself in front of that Latina QT you've invited for dinner, do you? The melted sugar should just be starting to smoke (the thinnest of wisps) and give off a slightly burnt smell when you take it off the heat to add the butter. Don't have the heat up to high. Be patient. It will be worth it, trust me.

Raw Egg Nationalism in Theory and Practice

As with salt and seasoning in general remember that you can always add more, but once you've added too much, you can't take it away. Just a couple of pinches of sea salt flakes will be enough. Hot salted caramel is hard to taste when it's in the pan.

You can also prepare the sauce beforehand and re-heat it.

For the caramel sauce you'll need:

- 200g granulated sugar
- 90g salted butter, cubed
- 120ml heavy cream
- A couple of pinches of good quality sea salt flakes

Heat the sugar in a saucepan over a medium heat. Stir constantly with a spatula or wooden soon. At first the sugar will clump, then it will melt into a caramel-coloured liquid as you continue stirring. Once the liquid has darkened (watch for those thin wisps of smoke and that hint of a burning smell), remove from the heat and add the butter. Return to the heat, stirring in the butter. Stir for about two minutes, then slowly pour in the cream while stirring. Allow the mixture to boil for a minute, then sprinkle in the sea salt. If you aren't serving the sauce directly from the pan, pour it into a heated serving jug to take to the table.

RAW EGG NATIONALIST'S BRIOCHE EGGY-BREAD BREAKFAST TOWER

I used to cook something like this during my short tenure as a chef in a hipster diner, and although I don't normally eat bread (or breakfast, at least not at the moment) just thinking about this recipe is making me very hungry. French toast – *pain perdu* to the French or eggy bread to us Brits – isn't usually made with brioche, a kind of sweet bread that sits in a happy middle ground between bread and pastry. Brioche is already overloaded with butter, eggs, milk and sugar, and then you go and soak slices of it in egg and fry them in butter… Hopefully you're getting an idea of how rich this recipe is. In Britain, at least, eggy bread is generally savoury rather than sweet; although there is a version called 'Poor Knights of Windsor' which contains sherry and is served with cinnamon sugar and jam. I don't dust the toast with sugar after it's cooked, but you can if you want. This version comes with crispy fried bacon, a

74

fried egg and maple syrup, but a variety of breakfast toppings will work: bacon and beans; bacon, beans and egg; bacon, sausage and egg; bacon, beans, sausage and egg. Or the slices of fried bread can simply be eaten on their own.

When assembling the tower, don't aspire to the heights of Western architecture. I suggest a simple double-decker arrangement: alternating a layer of bread with the fried egg, then more bread, then the bacon.

- 2 one-inch-thick slices of brioche bread (preferably a little stale)
- 2 whole eggs (1 for soaking the bread and 1 for frying)
- Thin bacon (as many slices as you fancy)
- Maple syrup
- 1 tbsp butter
- Salt and pepper

Cut each slice of brioche into three fingers. Break one of the eggs into a bowl and whisk it for a second. Add three fingers of brioche to the bowl at a time and leave to soak for a minute, before turning them and soaking for another minute. Remove from the bowl and repeat with the remaining three fingers. Heat the butter in a skillet on a medium heat and then fry the fingers for about a minute on each side, season and then reserve them on a warm plate. Fry the bacon and the other egg to your liking. Assemble the eggy-bread fingers, fried egg and the bacon, and drizzle with maple syrup.

BEN BRADDOCK'S LEFTOVER EGG-WHITE MERINGUES

If you've made Ben's frozen peach custard, you'll have eight egg whites left over. Instead of following the gymbro formula of rationing yourself to eating one a day for the next eight days, make two batches of meringues instead. You don't even have to eat them yourself; give them to a cute girl instead – or two. These are French meringues, by the way.

Makes one batch.

- 4 egg whites
- 300g granulated sugar

Preheat the oven to 215F, with a rack in the middle of the oven. Line a baking sheet with parchment and set aside. Whisk the egg whites by hand or with a mixer until soft peaks begin to form. Then add the sugar into the whites in four or five batches, mixing constantly, until stiff, glossy peaks begin to form. The mix is ready when a peak will form and hold its shape when the whisk is removed; the tip will fold back on itself. You can either pipe the meringues onto the parchment, or use a large spoon. Make sure there is space between the blobs of mixture on the parchment sheet. Bake for 60-90 minutes, until the outside is crisp. I tend to prefer a slightly chewier, more-marshmallow-y internal texture, but you can cook the meringues longer for a drier texture. The meringues should peel off the parchment easily. Turn off the oven and leave them to cool inside it, with the door open.

ALCOHOL

Alcohol

I won't lecture you on alcohol consumption. Unless you have a bad history with alcohol and find it safer not to drink at all, the occasional drink won't harm you. I never drink at home when I'm alone, but I try not to be a prig about drinking and I'd never sit drinking tap water if I'd cooked a nice girl something like a boeuf bourguignon or coq au vin.

The raw egg nationalist will, however, give beer a wide berth. Hops are one of the most powerful phytoestrogens known to science; I'm sure you already know this. Gruit, on the other hand, is beer as it used to be made, before the addition of hops, which allowed the once quickly perishable beer to be preserved for longer and therefore transported greater distances. Gruit is flavoured with other botanicals, such as rosemary, lavender, wormwood, heather, mugwort, lemon balm and juniper. Some are quite foul, but others are very nice. Big surprise there's something of a hipster gruit scene going on. (A very powerful and very dangerous form of gruit can be made with henbane, which was supposedly a common ingredient in witches' potions. In sufficient quantity – something like 20 leaves – it's fatal. Henbane gruit is said to be hallucinogenic, but in a very unpleasant way, and likely to induce a form of mania that will

80

see you remove all of your clothes and start masturbating in front of all and sundry, before attempting to claw your own eyes out. Be careful.)

Need I add that the cocktail recipes below all contain eggs in some form?

EGGNOG

Eggnog tastes better the longer in advance you make it, up to a week or more. This is a recipe that will serve 16, perhaps a local raw egg nationalist chapter meeting. Just divide the quantities by four if you want to make a more manageable quantity.

For the eggnog:

- 12 large egg yolks, with the whites reserved
- 400g granulated sugar
- 1ltr bourbon
- 1ltr whole milk
- 250ml heavy cream
- 200ml cognac or brandy

Alcohol

- 100ml dark rum
- pinch of salt

To serve:

- 12 egg whites
- 350ml heavy cream
- nutmeg

If you're going to make the eggnog well in advance, freeze the egg whites until the day before you're going to serve it. Combine the yolks and sugar in a large bowl and whisk until creamy. Add the remaining eggnog ingredients, stir to combine and then refrigerate the mixture for between one and three weeks (you can bottle it if you want). Thaw the egg whites in the fridge the day before you're going to serve the eggnog. Once they've thawed whisk them by hand or using a mixer until stiff peaks form, then add to a punch bowl. Whisk the cream until soft peaks form and then pour into the punch bowl. Stir the refrigerated mixture to recombine it and then add it to the whites and cream in the punch bowl, whisking gently to ensure incorporation (if you whisk too hard, you'll deflate the eggnog). Serve in cups with grated nutmeg as a garnish.

SNOWBALL

Similar to eggnog, but much simpler to make. The snowball contains Advocaat, a Dutch liqueur made with egg yolks, sugar, brandy and vanilla.

- 50ml Advocaat
- 25ml lime cordial or fresh lime juice
- 150ml lemonade
- Maraschino cherry

Shake the Advocaat and lime cordial or juice together with ice, then strain into a coupe or martini glass and top up with lemonade. Serve with a maraschino cherry on a cocktail stick.

NEGRONI FLIP

Almost any classic cocktail can be made into a 'flip' with the addition of an egg. The Negroni, named after an Italian count, is an acquired taste, and while you might think a Negroni with an egg in it would be disgusting, the egg takes the edge off the Campari and makes it something more akin to a thick cough syrup or medicinal milkshake.

- 25ml gin
- 25ml Campari
- 25ml sweet vermouth
- 10ml sugar syrup (dissolve demerara sugar in an equal volume of water)
- 1 whole egg
- Ice
- Orange peel to garnish

Combine the ingredients in a cocktail shaker, adding the egg last. Add ice and shake hard, for at least 30 seconds. Strain into a glass and add orange peel to garnish.

RAW EGG NATIONALIST'S COFFEE FLIP

My signature variation on a coffee flip has an extra whole yolk at the bottom of the glass. The bourbon and espresso can be replaced with a coffee liqueur should you prefer.

- 50 ml bourbon
- 1 shot of hot espresso (25ml)
- 15ml sugar syrup (dissolve demerara sugar in an equal volume of water)
- 1 whole egg
- 1 egg yolk
- 3 ice cubes

Put the egg yolk in a chilled coupe or martini glass. Combine all the remaining ingredients in a cocktail shaker and shake until the ice cubes have disappeared. Strain into the chilled glass.

PRAIRIE OYSTER

Really, this is a hangover cure, like a bloody Mary. Somewhere I read that, for ultimate efficacy, this should be consumed with fried pig's trotters. If you don't have any trotters to hand, try plenty of bacon and black pudding, or my eggy-bread tower.

- 1 whole egg
- 25ml vodka
- 1 dash vinegar
- 2tsp Worcestershire sauce
- 1tsp ketchup
- 2 dashes Tabasco
- Pinch of salt and pepper

Crack the egg into a glass, then add the rest of the ingredients. Drink in one go.

Printed in Great Britain
by Amazon